THE SCIENCE DETECTIVE INVESTIGATES

Electricity

Harriet McGregor

WAYLAND

First published in 2010 by Wayland

Copyright © Wayland 2010

Wayland
338 Euston Road
London NW1 3BH

Wayland Australia
Level 17/207 Kent Street
Sydney NSW 2000

Produced for Wayland by
White-Thomson Publishing Ltd

www.wtpub.co.uk
+44 (0)845 362 8240

Senior editor: Camilla Lloyd
Designer: Simon Borrough
Consultant: Jon Turney
Picture researcher: Amy Sparks
Illustrator: Stefan Chabluk
Sherlock Bones artwork: Richard Hook

British Library Cataloguing in Publication Data:
McGregor, Harriet.
   Electricity. – (The science detective investigates)
   1. Electricity–Juvenile literature. 2. Electricity–
   Experiments–Juvenile literature.
   I. Title II. Series
   537-dc22

ISBN 978 0 7502 6017 6

Printed in China

Wayland is a division of Hachette Children's Books, an Hachette UK company.

www.hachette.co.uk

Picture Acknowledgments:
Abbreviations: t-top, b-bottom, l-left, r-right, m-middle, c-centre.
Cover: Shutterstock (3imediaphoto)
Insides: Folios Shutterstock (Jim Barber): **1** Dreamstime (Bosenok); **4** Dreamstime (tl Jocic, tlc Paul George Bodea, trc Adrian Coroama, tr Charles Brutlag, bl Mike Tan, br Kingjon); **5** Corbis (Darryl Bush/San Francisco); **6** Dreamstime (Mangia); **7** Dreamstime (Bright); **9** Corbis (The Art Archive); **10** Getty (Greg Ceo); **13** Corbis (Andrew Lichtenstein); **15** Dreamstime (Bosenok); **16** Dreamstime (tr Nexus7, bl Gsermek, bc Vtorous, br Josefbosak); **17** Shutterstock (Jim Barber); **19** Dreamstime (Witr); **20** (l) Istockphoto (John Blair), **20** (r) Dreamstime (Cammeraydave); **21** Dreamstime (Edward Bock); **22** Alamy (isifa Image Service s.r.o.); **23** Photolibrary; **26** Shutterstock (3imediaphoto); **27** Photolibrary.

Contents

What is electricity?   4

Where does electricity come from?   6

Why do we need batteries?   8

How does electricity flow?   10

When does the flow of electricity stop?   12

Why do we use circuits?   14

What are conductors?   16

What are insulators?   18

What are switches?   20

How can you change a circuit?   22

Why do we use electrical symbols?   24

Is our use of electricity harming the environment?   26

Your project: How does the thickness of wire change a bulb's brightness?   28

Glossary   30

Answers   31

Websites   31

Index   32

Words that appear in **bold** can be found in the glossary on page 30.

The Science Detective, Sherlock Bones, will help you learn all about Electricity. The answers to Sherlock's questions can be found on page 31.

What is electricity?

We use electricity in countless ways every day. An electric alarm clock might wake us up in the morning, we switch on an electric light and go to the bathroom. We might use an electric toothbrush and then make breakfast using a toaster. Electricity can keep our homes warm and our showers hot. Electricity is even needed to start cars, and to power computers, phones and televisions.

▲ These devices all need electrical energy to make them work.

Energy

Electricity is a type of **energy**. Energy is the ability to do **work**. Humans get energy from food and **oxygen**. Food is digested inside our bodies and gives us energy to move, think, speak and grow.

Electrical energy makes bulbs light, washing machines spin and heaters give out heat. In each of these devices, electrical energy is turned into another type of energy. Light bulbs give out light energy, washing machines turn electrical energy into movement energy, and heaters produce heat energy.

THE SCIENCE DETECTIVE INVESTIGATES:

Using electricity

You will need:
• notebook • pen

Investigate how many times you use electricity in one day. As you go through your day, pay close attention to what you are doing. Make notes each time you use electricity. Write down the time, the type of electrical device and the purpose of the device. At the end of the day, count the number of times you used electricity. You might be surprised.

STAY SAFE

Although electricity can be very dangerous, there are ways to keep safe.

- Never use electrical devices near sources of water, such as the bath, sink or shower.
- Never touch electrical devices with wet hands.
- Never play with electrical plugs, switches and cables.
- Stay away from overhead power lines and pylons.
- Do not play outside during a thunderstorm.
- Look out for the symbols that warn you of the dangers of electricity.
- Stay away from electrified railway tracks.

There are lots of types of energy. Can you think of five? See if you can take this total to ten by doing an Internet search.

▼ The games console and the user need energy to play the game. The game needs electrical energy and the user needs energy from food.

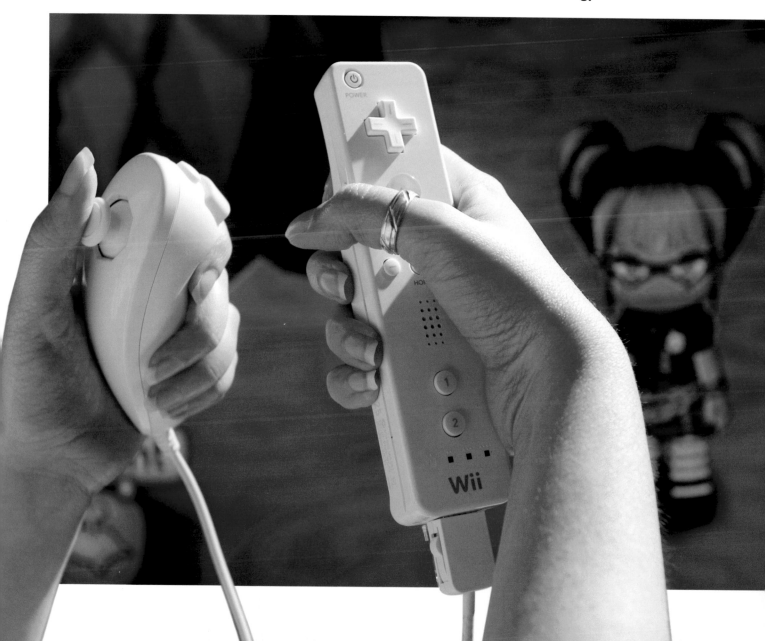

Where does electricity come from?

All electrical devices get their energy to work from either **mains electricity** or **batteries**. Televisions and microwaves plug into a wall socket. They use mains electricity. The electricity travels from the wall socket, down the cable and into the device. Electrical energy makes the device work.

Electricity's journey

Most mains electricity comes from huge factories called **power stations**. In a power station, a **fuel** is burned. The fuel is often natural gas or coal. The burning fuel heats water. Steam from the water turns large fans called **turbines**. The turbines spin a **generator** which makes electricity. In power stations, the energy in fuel is turned into electrical energy. **Alternative energy**, such as wind and solar energy, can also be made into electricity (see page 27).

SCIENCE AT WORK

Not all electricity comes from power stations and batteries. Lightning is a type of electricity called **static electricity**. It is produced in clouds during thunderstorms. When enough static electricity builds up in clouds, it jumps either to the ground or to another cloud. We see the bolt of lightning and hear a bang of thunder. The thunder is caused by the lightning heating the air very suddenly.

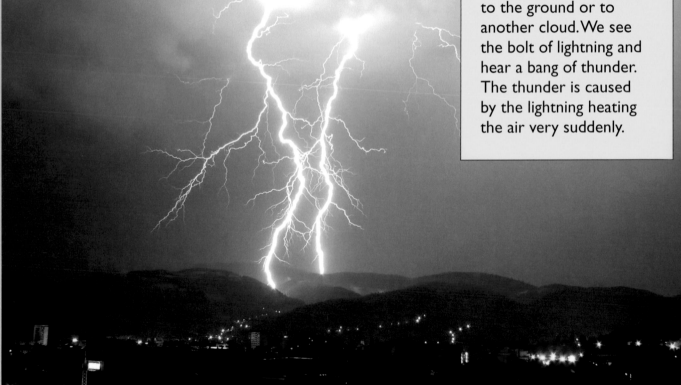

▲ **Lightning has a temperature of around 28,000°C (50,000°F), which is approximately five times hotter than the surface of the Sun.**

Electricity travels to homes and schools along heavy cables. The cables run underground in cities, but overground in open areas. Large pylons hold the cables high above ground. Pylons are very tall, metal towers.

The electricity carried by overhead cables is extremely powerful. It is important that pylons hold the cables high above ground because anyone touching the cable could be killed by an **electric shock**.

▲ **Electricity is carried overground and underground in thick, heavy cables in this residential area.**

Why do we need batteries?

Batteries are useful **power sources** because they are portable (easy to carry around) and come in all shapes and sizes. Watches, calculators and hearing aids use tiny button batteries. Torches use different-sized batteries, depending on the size of the torch.

Energy from batteries

Batteries are stores of energy. They contain chemicals. Each battery has a positive and a negative terminal. Electricity is produced when a wire is connected to the positive and negative terminals of the battery. The electricity flows from the negative terminal, through the wire and back to the positive terminal.

THE SCIENCE DETECTIVE INVESTIGATES:

Match the battery

Look carefully at the batteries shown in the pictures. Which battery is found in which of the following devices?

Remote control

Mobile phone

Watch

Car

1

2

3

4

Battery life

A battery's energy store does not last forever. Battery life depends on the device that it powers. Some devices need more electricity than others. These devices make a battery run down quickly.

Mobile phones and some cameras use small batteries that can be **recharged** by plugging them into an electric socket for a short time. This means that they can be used again and again. Some wind-up radios and torches contain rechargeable batteries. When they are wound up, the battery is recharged.

The types of battery in small torches are safe to use in investigations. Button batteries and car batteries are not safe to use. You should never take apart any type of battery.

▼ The voltaic pile was the first battery to produce a continuous supply of electricity.

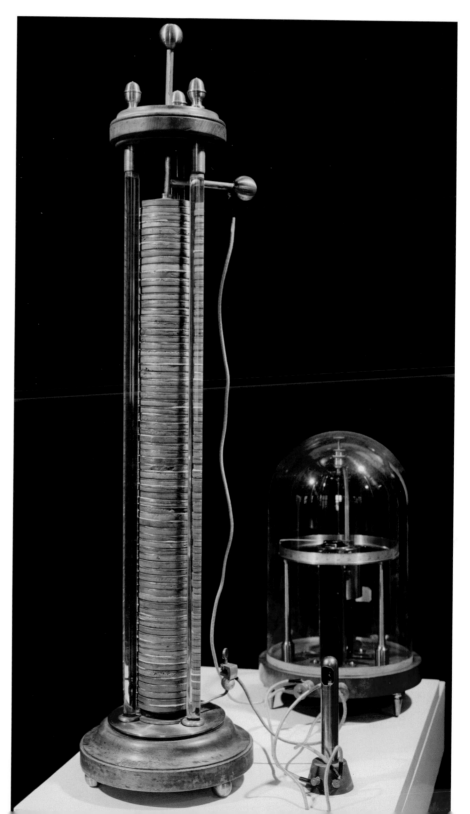

SCIENCE AT WORK

Alessandro Volta invented the first battery in 1799. It was called the voltaic pile. It was made of piles of copper and zinc discs, separated by pieces of flannel soaked in a chemical solution.

How does electricity flow?

Flowing electricity is called an **electrical current**. You can think of a current of electricity as flowing water. Imagine a loop of pipes filled with water. To make the water flow, you need a pump. To make an electrical current flow, you need a power source.

◀ **A tap pushes the water through the hose pipe. A battery or mains socket supplies the electricity which then flows along wires.**

🐾 **If flowing water represents an electrical current, what do the pipes represent?**

Circuits

A **circuit** is a path around which electricity flows. The different parts of a circuit are called the **components**. The main components of a simple circuit are the power source, wires and the device to be powered. Circuits must be complete and have no gaps. If there is a gap, the current will not flow and the device will not work.

Power sources

Batteries are usually used as the power source in simple circuits. In larger circuits, mains electricity is the power source. Wires form the path along which electricity flows. When electricity flows through a device, it gives it energy and the device begins to work.

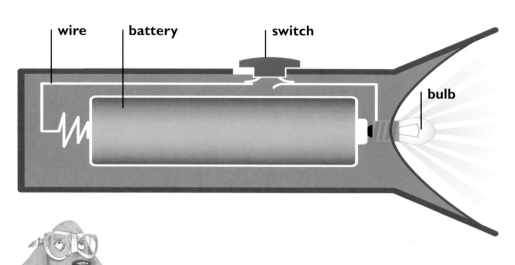

wire　battery　switch

bulb

◀ Inside a torch, a battery pushes an electrical current around a circuit to light the bulb.

THE SCIENCE DETECTIVE INVESTIGATES:

Make a circuit

You will need:
- 2 wires • battery • light bulb

Look closely at the items shown here. How would you connect them to make a circuit?

1　Use one wire to connect one battery terminal to the light bulb.

2　Use the second wire to connect the other battery terminal to the other side of the light bulb. Is your circuit complete? Does the bulb light?

3　Draw your circuit and label each of the components. Make sure you label the negative and positive terminals. Draw an arrow to show which direction the electrical current flows (see page 8).

When does the flow of electricity stop?

Circuits do not always work as they should, especially if there is a gap in the circuit. Use the information below and your detective skills to work out why a circuit might not work.

1

2

3

Problems in a circuit

There are a number of things that could be wrong if there is a problem in a circuit. To find out what is wrong, first check the components – the power source, wires and the device. Check that the circuit is complete. Do all the wires connect securely with the other components? If the circuit is complete, insert a fresh battery to check whether the battery has run down. If this does not solve the problem, look closely at the device to see whether it has been damaged. Try replacing the device if it looks damaged.

Short circuits

A **short circuit** is an unwanted connection in a circuit. Electricity always takes the easiest route. If there are two loops of wire in a circuit, and only one loop contains a device, the electricity will not travel along the loop with the device. Loose connections in a circuit make a short circuit more likely.

Water forms short circuits. It is dangerous to operate anything electrical with wet hands. The electricity may travel through you instead of through the circuit. Electric shocks can kill.

4

🐾 Look closely at the four circuits on this page. In which of these circuits should the bulb light?

SCIENCE AT WORK

When the mains electricity supply fails, we say a **power cut** has happened. This happens for many different reasons. Extreme weather, such as hurricanes or heatwaves, can damage overhead power cables. Old equipment, vandalism (deliberate damage caused by people), fire and lightning strikes can also cause power cuts.

▼ In 2003, one of the world's biggest power cuts affected more than 50 million people in the United States and Canada. In New York City, these people had to walk home from work because the subway (underground train) does not work without electricity.

Why do we use circuits?

Circuits let us use electricity. They connect the lights in schools, the wall sockets of a house and the electrical systems in a car. They are present in remote controls, computers, traffic lights, fridges and all other electrical devices. Computer **microchips** have tiny circuits. Office buildings contain large circuits. Circuits can even be the size of a whole country.

Series and parallel circuits

A **series circuit** is one loop of wire with components connected in it. The electricity travels from the battery, along the wire, and through every component before it returns to the battery. Imagine a series circuit that contains one power source and many fairy light bulbs. If any of the light bulbs blow, the circuit will no longer work and none of the bulbs will light. The blown light bulb creates a gap in the circuit and the electricity is stopped from flowing.

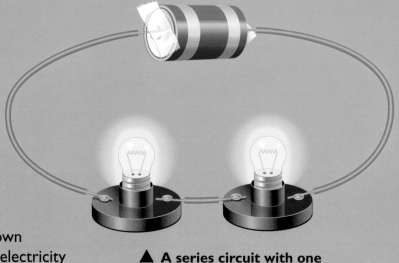

▲ **A series circuit with one battery and two bulbs.**

A **parallel circuit** has more than one loop of wire. In a parallel circuit, the electricity leaves the battery and then splits to travel down more than one loop of wire. Imagine a parallel circuit with two loops of wire. Each loop of wire carries one light bulb. If one of the bulbs blows, electricity can still carry on around the other loop and light the bulb.

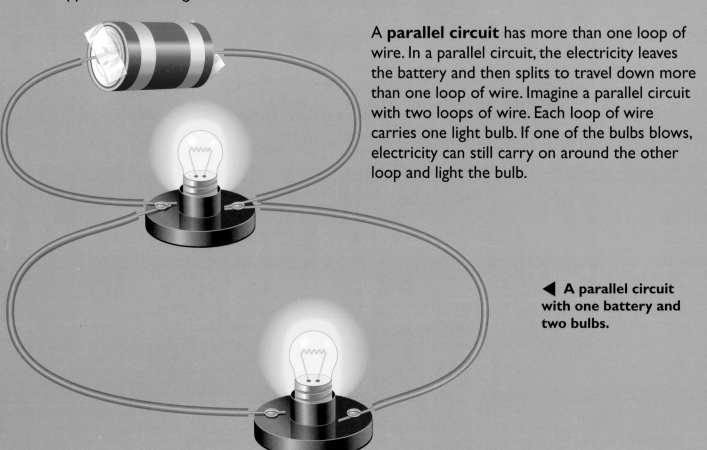

◀ **A parallel circuit with one battery and two bulbs.**

The national grid

In the UK, almost every building, street light and traffic signal is connected in a huge circuit. This circuit is called the **national grid**. When electricity leaves power stations, it enters the power cables that make up the national grid. The electricity is very powerful and has a high **voltage**. As it travels through the power cables, its voltage is changed. By the time it reaches your house, the voltage is much lower, although it is still powerful enough to be very dangerous.

▲ **Skyscraper lights are connected in parallel. At night, the lights on a whole floor can be turned off, while the lights on other floors can stay lit.**

What are conductors?

Conductors are materials that allow electricity to pass through them easily. They conduct electricity. Metals are good conductors. Some materials do not let electricity pass through them easily. These materials are poor conductors. Most non-metals are poor conductors.

Good conductors and poor conductors

Copper, aluminium, iron, steel and graphite are good electrical conductors. Graphite is found in the 'lead' of a pencil. Water can also conduct electricity. Plastic, rubber, wood and glass are poor electrical conductors.

Circuits and conductors

In a circuit, it is important that some of the materials conduct electricity. Electrical wires contain thin strands of copper metal wound tightly together. The copper carries the electricity around the circuit.

Conductors are also used in other parts that make up the circuit. Some light bulbs contain a very thin wire made from tungsten metal, called a **filament**. Electricity can pass through the filament, but not as easily as it can pass through the copper wire. When electricity travels through the filament, it heats the tungsten and makes it glow brightly.

◄ ▲ **Steel (far left), copper (below), graphite (pencil 'lead') and water conduct electricity.**

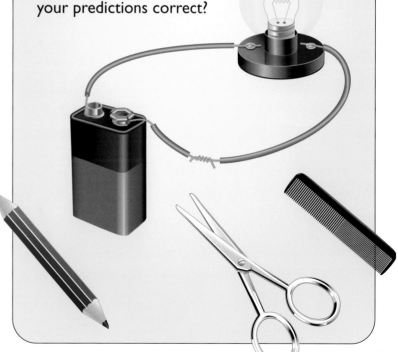

THE SCIENCE DETECTIVE INVESTIGATES:

Find the conductors

You will need:
• 3 wires • light bulb • battery • test objects including something made from metal and from plastic

Look at the circuit below. The bulb will light because it is connected to a battery in a complete circuit. What will happen if other objects are added into the circuit? Look at the everyday objects collected by the scientist. Predict whether or not the circuit will work with each of these objects connected in it.

Make the circuit and connect up each item in turn in the circuit. What happens to the light bulb when the circuit contains a good conductor? What happens to the light bulb when the circuit contains a poor conductor? Were your predictions correct?

🐾 **Light bulbs that have filaments are called incandescent light bulbs. Look up incandescence on the Internet to find out why this adjective is used to describe these light bulbs.**

What are insulators?

An **insulator** is a material that does not allow electricity to pass through it. Insulators do not conduct electricity. Plastic, glass, wood and rubber are insulators.

Insulators and circuits

In a circuit, insulators are just as important as conductors. Insulators help to make sure the electricity only flows where we want it. A plug carries electricity from the mains socket into a wire to power a device. The metal pins of the plug conduct electricity. The casing of the plug is made from plastic or rubber, which are insulators. This makes it safe to hold the plug. The copper wire (a conductor) is covered with plastic (an insulator) to make sure the electricity reaches the device and does not take a short cut.

THE SCIENCE DETECTIVE INVESTIGATES:

Find the insulators

Draw a table with three headings: Object, Material, Conductor or Insulator. Collect together some household objects, such as cutlery, pens, erasers and books. What is each object made from? If you don't know, use the Internet or reference books to find out. Predict whether or not each object can conduct electricity. Fill in your table. What conclusions can you draw from this investigation?

◀ ▲ **Plugs look different around the world. They can have two or three pins. All plugs are cased by an insulator.**

Where else are insulators useful?

Look at any electrical device and you will see that there is an insulator on it somewhere. A light bulb is surrounded by glass, a torch is surrounded by plastic, and **switches** are made from plastic even if they have a metal outer surface.

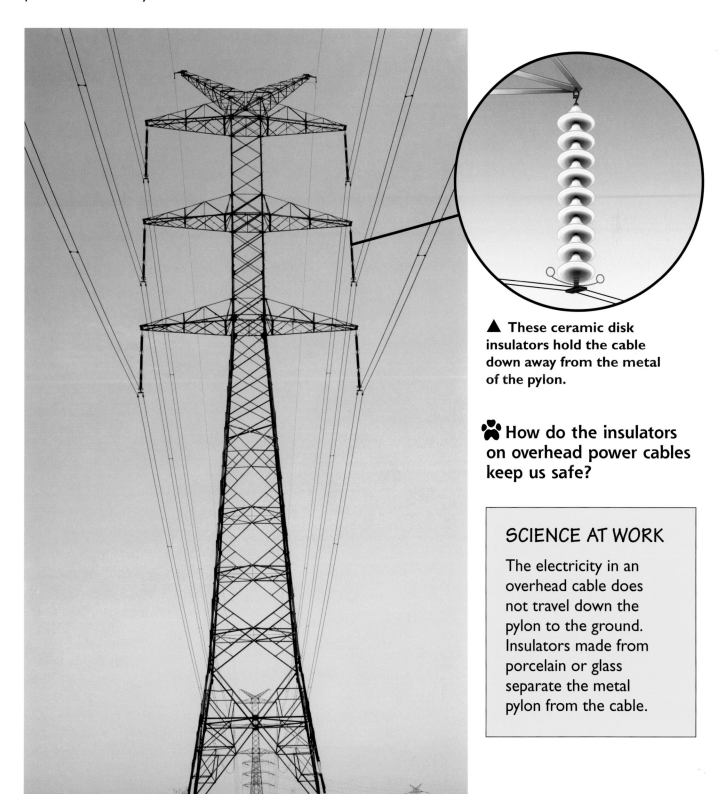

▲ These ceramic disk insulators hold the cable down away from the metal of the pylon.

🐾 How do the insulators on overhead power cables keep us safe?

SCIENCE AT WORK

The electricity in an overhead cable does not travel down the pylon to the ground. Insulators made from porcelain or glass separate the metal pylon from the cable.

What are switches?

A switch stops or starts the flow of electricity in a circuit. Switches give us control over the flow of electricity. Look around the room at the electrical devices and you will see that each one has a switch.

How switches work

To turn on an electrical device such as a hairdryer, you push the switch. It completes a circuit, electricity flows and the hairdryer works. To turn off the hairdryer you push the switch in the opposite direction. This breaks the circuit, the flow of electricity stops and the hairdryer turns off.

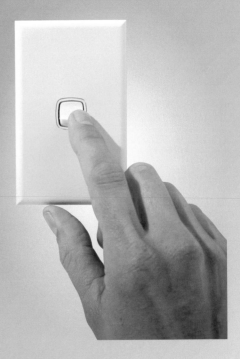

▲ Pressing a switch stops or starts the flow of electricity.

Switch off

Using switches saves electricity and money. Each time a light or machine is switched off completely it stops using electricity. Using electricity costs money, and by switching off devices you save money.

◀ Switches on a hairdryer turn it on and off.

THE SCIENCE DETECTIVE INVESTIGATES:

Make a switch

You will need:
- 3 wires • battery • light bulb
- 2 drawing pins • piece of wood • paper clip

Follow the method below to make a circuit that contains a switch.

1 Use a wire to connect the battery to the light bulb.

2 Connect the second wire to the other terminal of the battery.

3 Connect the third wire to the other connection of the light bulb.

4 Push one drawing pin into the wood.

5 Hook the paper clip over the head of the drawing pin.

6 Push the other drawing pin into the wood near the first drawing pin. Make sure the paper clip can reach it but don't connect it to the paper clip.

7 Use the loose end of the wire to connect the light bulb to one of the drawing pins.

8 Use the other loose wire to connect the battery to the other drawing pin.

9 Now touch the paper clip to the drawing pin. What happens?

10 Move the paper clip away from the drawing pin. What happens this time? Which part of your equipment is the switch? Explain what is happening as you move the paper clip.

◀ **MP3 players have switches to turn them off. Otherwise, the battery would run down very quickly.**

How can you change a circuit?

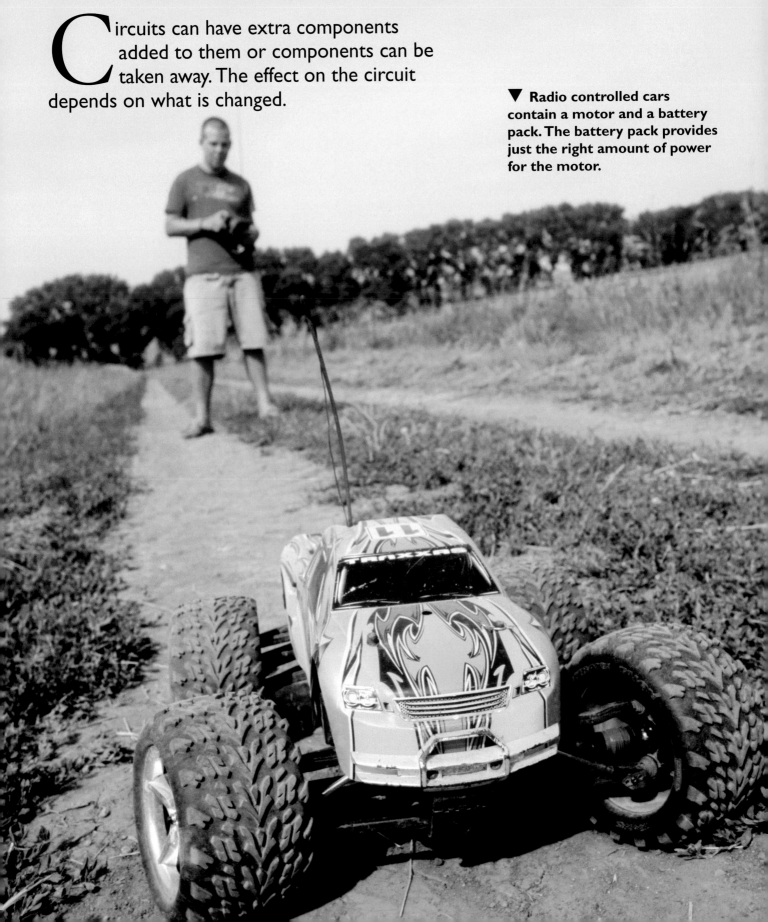

Circuits can have extra components added to them or components can be taken away. The effect on the circuit depends on what is changed.

▼ **Radio controlled cars contain a motor and a battery pack. The battery pack provides just the right amount of power for the motor.**

▲ The electric eel lives on the muddy bottoms of rivers in South America. It can give an electrical shock of up to 500 volts.

SCIENCE AT WORK

Electric fish can make electricity. They use it to stun their prey, navigate their way through the water, communicate with other fish or detect objects in the water. Usually, an electric organ in the tail of the fish makes the electricity. The bolts of electricity can give a nasty shock.

Brighter and faster

When extra batteries are added to a circuit, the device works harder – the motor runs more quickly or the bulb glows more brightly. Be careful not to add too many batteries. Bulbs and motors are designed to be used with batteries of a certain voltage. If the voltage of the batteries is too great, the device may burn out. For example, a 1.5 volt bulb needs a 1.5 volt battery. Taking away batteries makes a motor run more slowly or makes a bulb glow less brightly.

Extra bulbs

As more bulbs are added to a circuit, they glow less brightly. In a circuit with one battery, two bulbs will glow less brightly than one bulb. The two bulbs will glow with the same level of brightness – one will not glow more brightly than the other.

Types of wire

Electricity finds it easier to travel through thick wire than through very thin wire. A thin wire provides more **resistance** to the flow of electricity. A bulb will glow less brightly in a circuit that contains very thin wire. It will glow more brightly in a circuit that contains thick wire. Lengthening the wire in a circuit can also make a bulb glow less brightly.

Why do we use electrical symbols?

Symbols are used to represent objects or give instructions. Road symbols tell drivers how fast they can drive or when to watch out for children crossing the road. Symbols on drinks cans tell us whether they can be recycled. In science, symbols are used to represent components of circuits.

Understanding circuits

Imagine if every member of your class drew a picture of a circuit, but without using symbols. Everyone would have their own way of drawing each component, and it might not be clear what each drawing represented. You would probably find it difficult to use the drawings to assemble the circuit. Symbols are much easier and quicker to draw. A symbol diagram of a circuit is usually far easier to understand and use.

▲ **This symbol warns that there is danger from electricity. You may have seen it near pylons.**

▼ **This circuit diagram represents the complex electrical circuit inside a stereo amplifier.**

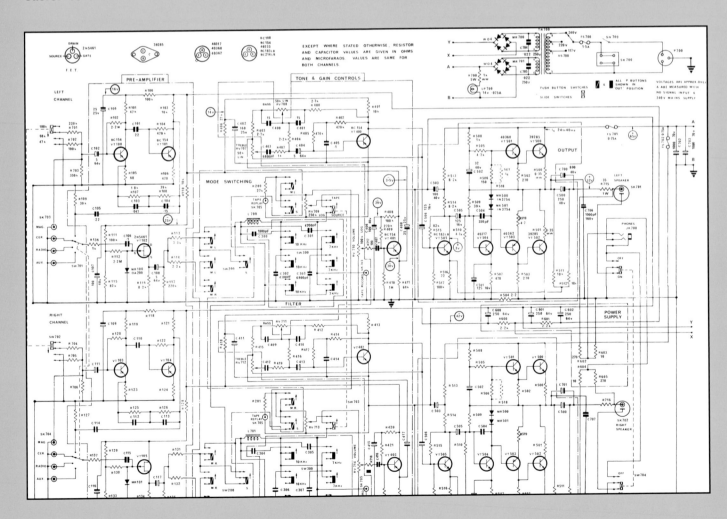

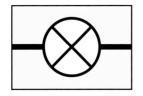

Bulb

Buzzer

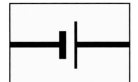

One battery

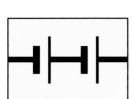 

Two batteries

Motor

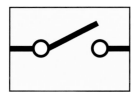

Switch off

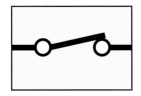

Switch on

Wire

Electrical symbols

These pictures show the most commonly used electrical symbols. To draw a circuit with symbols, replace each component with the relevant symbol. Link the components together with a straight line (the symbol for wire). Make sure there are no gaps in the circuit and remember every circuit needs a power source.

▼ **This circuit contains wire, two batteries, a buzzer and a switch.**

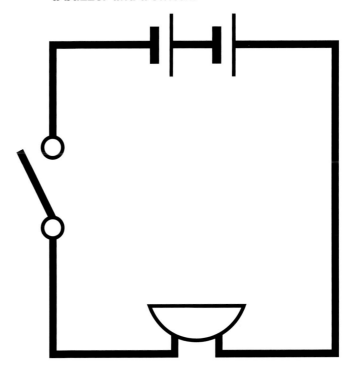

Is our use of electricity harming the environment?

When **fossil fuels** are burned to make electricity, carbon dioxide gas is released into the air. Carbon dioxide is a **greenhouse gas**. It collects in the atmosphere, trapping heat around the Earth and causing global warming. Global warming may lead to climate change.

Climate change

The climate is the long-term weather in a particular area. For example, the climate at the North Pole is very cold, and the climate in the Sahara desert is hot and dry. Climates naturally change over hundreds of years, but scientists believe that burning fossil fuels is changing them faster. If the climate warms, polar ice caps may melt and sea levels may rise. Animals and plants may not be able to adapt to the new conditions. Global warming and climate change may lead to extreme weather events and widespread flooding. It may even cause the extinction (dying out) of many species.

▶ **Modern low-energy light bulbs use less electricity than incandescent light bulbs. Using less electricity means burning less fuel. This may help to prevent climate change.**

Alternative energy

Solar energy (the energy in sunlight) can be changed into electricity in solar panels. Wind energy can be captured by wind turbines and made into electricity. The energy in moving water can also be harnessed to make electricity. Despite these advances in technology, most electricity is still made by burning fossil fuels. Electricity from alternative sources has so far been more expensive to make than from burning fossil fuels.

How can we help?

Switching off electrical devices can help to save the planet. The less electricity we use, the less carbon dioxide is created. Make sure your television or computer is turned off and not left on standby, and switch off lights when they are not in use.

How does reducing car travel help the environment?

▼ Electric cars do not burn fuel and do not release carbon dioxide into the atmosphere. Unfortunately, the electricity they use may have been made by burning fossil fuels.

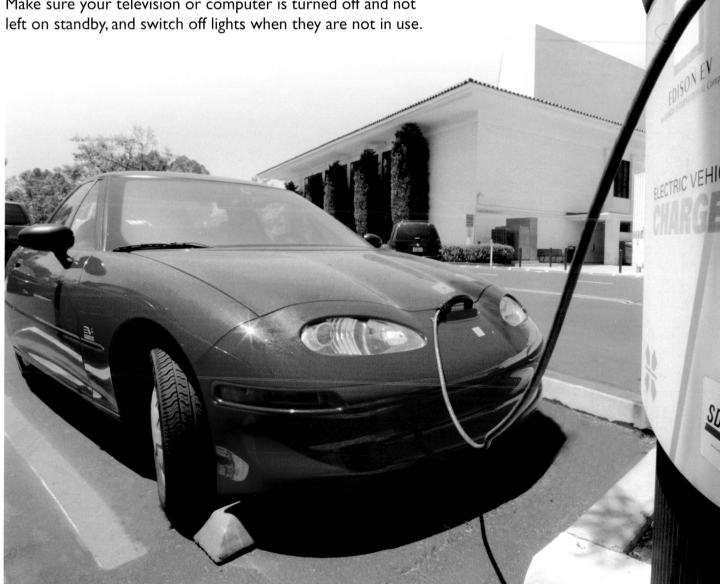

Your project: How does the thickness of wire change a bulb's brightness?

I f a very thin wire is connected in a circuit, what effect will this have on a light bulb? First, make a prediction about what you think might happen. In this case, the prediction could be: *Thin wire added to a circuit will change the brightness of the bulb.* Use the information below to carry out your own investigation.

Hypothesis

A hypothesis is a statement about what you think might happen in your investigation. For this experiment it could be: *In a circuit with one battery and one bulb, a thin wire added to the circuit causes the bulb to glow less brightly.*

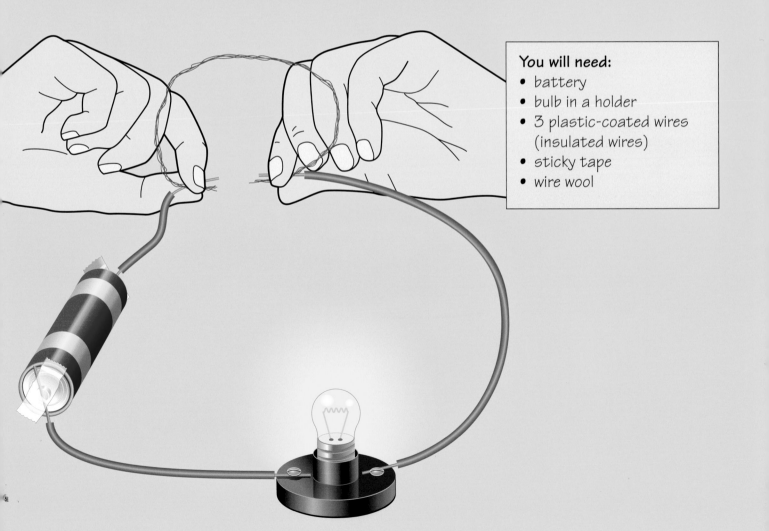

You will need:
- battery
- bulb in a holder
- 3 plastic-coated wires (insulated wires)
- sticky tape
- wire wool

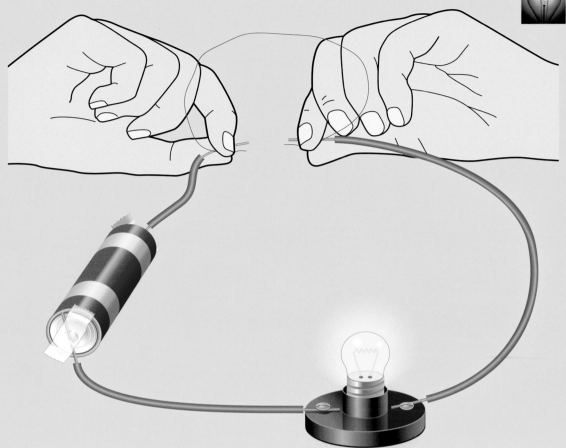

Method

1 Use sticky tape to connect one wire to the positive terminal of the battery and another wire to the negative terminal of the battery.

2 Connect the bulb to one of the battery wires. Attach the third wire to the other side of the bulb.

3 Unravel some of the wire wool to make a strand of wire. It should be roughly as thick as your insulated wires.

4 Hold the wire that you have made so that it is touching the two loose ends of the insulated wires to complete the circuit.

5 Look at the bulb. Is it glowing?

6 Make the wire wool thinner by removing some of the strands.

7 Connect it back into the circuit and look at the bulb. Is it brighter or dimmer?

8 Make the wire wool even thinner and connect it into the circuit again. Is the bulb brighter or dimmer?

A fair test is one in which only one part of an investigation is changed at a time. Is your method a fair test? If it is, how do you know this? What is your conclusion?

What happened and why?

Your results should show that as the wire wool strand is made thinner and thinner, the light bulb glows less brightly. Electricity finds it hard to travel through thin wires. They provide resistance. When the wire is very thin, only a small electrical current (a small amount of electricity) travels around the circuit. The bulb cannot glow brightly with such a small electrical current.

Glossary

alternative energy Energy that comes from sources that do not harm the environment, and that do not use up non-renewable natural resources. Solar and wind energy are alternative energy sources.

battery A portable device that contains chemicals and produces electricity.

circuit A complete loop around which electricity flows.

component A part of an electrical circuit.

conductor A material that allows electricity to pass through it.

electric shock When electricity passes through the body causing damage.

electrical current A flow of electricity.

energy The ability to do work.

filament A part in some types of light bulbs that glows when electricity passes through it.

fossil fuels Coal, oil and natural gas are fossil fuels. They are formed underground over millions of years.

fuel A material that is used to provide energy.

generator A machine that creates electricity.

greenhouse gases Gases such as carbon dioxide and methane that build up in the atmosphere and trap heat.

insulator A material that does not allow electricity to pass through it.

mains electricity Electricity that is supplied to homes, offices and schools through a grid system.

microchip A piece of material that contains a tiny circuit.

national grid A network of power cables that links together power stations, cities, towns and villages.

oxygen A type of gas found in the air.

parallel circuit An electrical circuit that has more than one loop of wire.

power cut When the mains electricity supply stops working.

power source A device or system that supplies electricity, such as mains electricity or a battery.

power station A large factory that makes electricity.

recharge To make a battery fill up with energy again.

resistance When something tries to slow down or stop the flow of electricity through a material.

series circuit An electrical circuit that consists of only one loop of wire.

short circuit An accidental connection between two points in a circuit.

static electricity Electricity that is not flowing.

switch A device that opens or closes a gap in an electrical circuit.

turbine A machine that can be turned by wind, water or steam.

voltage A measure of electricity.

work When a force acts and moves an object, work is done.

Answers

Page 4: Everyone will use different electrical items throughout their day. For example, you may have an electrical alarm clock that wakes you up in the morning, you might listen to the radio on the way to school and use a computer in class.

Page 5: There are many types of energy such as: electrical, mechanical, movement, stored, light, heat, nuclear, chemical, sound, and gravitational energy.

Page 8: Remote control = 3, Mobile phone = 2, Watch = 1, Car = 4.

Page 10: If flowing water represents electrical current, the pipes represent the wires.

Page 11: If you have followed the directions correctly, the circuit should be complete and the bulb should light. The arrow should show that the electricity moves away from the negative terminal and towards the positive terminal.

Page 12: Circuit 1 will not work because it has no battery. Circuit 2 will not work because there is only one connection to the light bulb. Circuit 3 is the only one in which the bulb will light. It is a complete circuit that contains a battery, and has wires connected to each side of the bulb and each terminal of the battery. Circuit 4 will not work because there is a gap in the circuit.

Page 17: Incandescence is when an object gets very hot and gives out light (glows). Incandescent light bulbs become hot and glow brightly when they are connected in a circuit.

Page 17: When the circuit contains a good conductor, the bulb lights. When the circuit contains a poor conductor, the bulb does not light.

Page 18: Household objects could include spoons, bottles, books, bags, pens and pencils. Metal objects, water and graphite (pencil 'lead') can conduct electricity. Wood, plastic, rubber and glass cannot conduct electricity.

Page 19: The insulators on overhead power cables keep us safe by preventing the electricity from travelling down the pylon where it could give someone an electric shock.

Page 21: When the paper clip touches the drawing pin, the bulb lights. When the paper clip is moved away from the drawing pin, the bulb goes out. The paper clip is the switch in your circuit. When it touches both drawing pins, it completes the circuit which allows electricity to flow around the circuit and through the light bulb. When you move it away, you create a gap in the circuit and electricity stops flowing.

Page 27: Reducing car travel helps the environment in several ways. Cars burn either diesel or petrol. These fuels are fossil fuels that are formed underground over millions of years. They are non-renewable, which means that once they are used up, we cannot replace them. Reducing car travel means using up less fossil fuels. When cars burn fuel, they release harmful chemicals into the air. The chemicals contribute to global warming, acid rain and health problems in humans. Reducing car travel will help to combat these problems.

Page 29: The method is a fair test. You are only changing the thickness of the wire. All the other parts of the circuit – the battery, insulated wires, bulb and the length of the thin wire – stay the same. Your conclusion should be that the thinner the wire, the less brightly the bulb glows. Thin wires provide more resistance than thick wires.

Page 29: The thinner the wire wool, the less electricity can flow around the circuit. The wire wool provides resistance to the electrical current and the bulb glows less brightly.

Websites

http://ksnn.larc.nasa.gov/webtext.cfm?unit=static electricity
Find out all about static electricity.

http://scifiles.larc.nasa.gov/text/kids/Problem_Board/problems/electricity/circuits2.html
Go to this NASA website to find out more about circuit diagrams, series circuits and parallel circuits.

http://www.bbc.co.uk/schools/ks2bitesize/science/activities/changing_circuits.shtml
Try this activity to investigate changing circuits.

http://www.bbc.co.uk/schools/ks2bitesize/science/activities/conductors.shtml
Carry out this activity to learn more about conductors and circuits.

http://www.eia.doe.gov/kids/energyfacts/
Lots of information about different types of energy.

http://www.energyquest.ca.gov/story/chapter02.html
Take a closer look at electricity and how it works.

http://www.hantsfire.gov.uk/circuits
An interactive animation about how circuits work.

Index

The numbers in **bold** refer to pictures

alternative energy 6, 27
aluminium 16

batteries 6, **8**, **9**, 10, **11**, **12**, **14**, 17, **21**, 22, 23, **25**, **28**, **29**
battery life 9
button batteries **8**, 9
buzzer **25**

chemicals 8, 9
circuits 10, **11**, **12**, **14**, 15, 16, **17**, 18, 20, **21**, 22, 23, **24**, **25**, **28**, **29**
   parallel **14**, 15
   series **14**
climate change 26
component 10, 11, 12, 14, 22, 24
computers 4, 14, 27
conductors **16**, 17, 18
copper 9, **16**, 18
current 10, 11, 29

electric cars **27**
electric fish **23**
electric shock 7, 23
energy 4, 5, 6, 8, 9, 10, 12, 27

fair test 29
fairy lights 14
filament 16, **17**
food 4
fuel 6, 26, 27

glass 16, 18, 19
global warming 26
graphite **16**
greenhouse gas 26

heat energy 4, 6, 16, 26
hypothesis 28

incandescence 17
insulators **18**, **19**, 28, 29

light bulb 4, **11**, **12**, **14**, 15, **17**, 19, **21**, 23, **25**, **26**, **28**, **29**
light energy 4
lightning **6**, 13
loose connections 12

mains electricity 6, 10, 13
microchips 14
microwave 6
motor 22, 23, **25**
movement energy 4

national grid 15

office buildings 14
overhead cables 5, 7, 13, **19**

plastic 16, 17, 18, 19
plugs 5, **18**
power cut **13**
power lines 5, **19**
power stations 6, 15
problem circuits 12
pylons 5, 7, **19**, 24

recharging 9
resistance 23, 29
rubber 16, 18

safety 5, 9, 19
short circuit 12, 18
skyscrapers **15**
solar energy 6, 27
static electricity 6
steel **16**
switches 5, **11**, 19, **20**, **21**, **25**
symbols 5, **24**, **25**

television 4, 6, 27
thunderstorms 5, **6**
torch 8, 9, **11**, 19
turbines 6

Volta, Alessandro 9
voltage 15, 23
voltaic pile **9**

wall socket 6, 9, 10, 14, 18
water 5, 6, 10, 12, **16**, 27
weather 13, 27
wet hands 5, 12
wind energy 6, 27
wood 16, 18
work 4

The Science Detective Investigates

Contents of titles in the series:

Electricity
978 0 7502 6017 6
What is electricity?
Where does electricity come from?
Why do we need batteries?
How does electricity flow?
When does the flow of electricity stop?
Why do we use circuits?
What are conductors?
What are insulators?
What are switches?
How can you change a circuit?
Why do we use electrical symbols?
Is our use of electricity harming the environment?
Your project: How does the length of wire change a bulb's brightness?

Forces and Motion
978 0 7502 6022 0
What are forces?
What are balanced forces?
How do forces change an object's shape?
How do forces change the way things move?
What is gravity?
What is friction?
What is air resistance?
What is water resistance?
Why do objects float and sink?
What is pressure?
How do we use forces?
What are levers and pulleys?
Your project: Investigating forces

Light
978 0 7502 6020 6
What is light?
What are natural sources of light?
What is artificial light?
How does light travel?
Which materials let light through?
What are shadows?
What is reflection?
How do we use light to see?
What is refraction?
What are lenses?
How do we use lenses?
How do we see colours?
Your project: Light in action

Magnets and Springs
978 0 7502 6019 0
What is magnetism?
Which materials are magnetic?
What is a magnetic field?
Is the Earth a magnet?
Are all magnets the same?
How do we use magnets?
How is magnetism used by trains?
What is a spring?
What happens when you stretch or compress a spring?
Why are spring loaded objects useful?
How are springs used in measuring?
How are springs used in suspension?
Your project: How can you make a compass?

Sound
978 0 7502 6021 3
What is sound?
How does sound travel?
How do humans hear?
How do other animals hear?
Are all sounds the same?
How do we make sounds with our voices?
What is music?
What is sound insulation?
What is an echo?
How is sound used?
How do we measure sound?
Are there sounds that humans cannot hear?
Your project: Which state of matter does sound travel through best?

Materials
978 0 7502 6018 3
What are materials?
How do we use materials?
What are solids and liquids?
What are gases?
What is evaporation?
What is condensation?
When do materials melt and freeze?
How does heat change materials?
What are mixtures and solutions?
Which materials can be squashed and stretched?
What are conductors and insulators?
What will materials be like in the future?
Your project: Testing materials

WAYLAND